How to be Brilliant at
WRITING POETRY

 Brilliant Publications

We hope you and your class enjoy using this book. Other books in the series include:

Science titles

How to be Brilliant at Recording in Science	978 1 897675 10 6
How to be Brilliant at Science Investigations	978 1 897675 11 3
How to be Brilliant at Materials	978 1 897675 12 0
How to be Brilliant at Electricity, Light and Sound	978 1 897675 13 7
How to be Brilliant at Living Things	978 1 897675 66 3

English titles

How to be Brilliant at Writing Stories	978 1 897675 00 7
How to be Brilliant at Grammar	978 1 897675 02 1
How to be Brilliant at Making Books	978 1 897675 03 8
How to be Brilliant at Spelling	978 1 897675 08 3
How to be Brilliant at Reading	978 1 897675 09 0
How to be Brilliant at Word Puzzles	978 1 897675 88 5

Maths titles

How to be Brilliant at Using a Calculator	978 1 897675 04 5
How to be Brilliant at Algebra	978 1 897675 05 2
How to be Brilliant at Numbers	978 1 897675 06 9
How to be Brilliant at Shape and Space	978 1 897675 07 6
How to be Brilliant at Mental Arithmetic	978 1 897675 21 2

History and Geography titles

How to be Brilliant at Recording in History	978 1 897675 22 9
How to be Brilliant at Recording in Geography	978 1 897675 31 1

Christmas title

How to be Brilliant at Christmas Time	978 1 897675 63 2

Published by Brilliant Publications,
Unit 10, Sparrow Hall Farm,
Edlesborough,
Dunstable,
Bedfordshire,
LU6 2ES

Sales and stock enquiries:
Tel: 01202 712910
Fax: 0845 1309300
e-mail:brilliant@bebc.co.uk
www.brilliantpublications.co.uk

General information enquiries:
Tel: 01525 222292
The name 'Brilliant Publications' and its logo are registered trademarks.

Written by Irene Yates
Illustrated by Kate Ford

Printed in the UK

© Irene Yates 1993
ISBN 978 1 897675 01 4

First published in 1993
Reprinted 1994, 1997, 1998, 1999, 2002, 2007
10 9 8 7

The right of Irene Yates to be identified as author of this work has been asserted by her in accordance with the Copyright, Designs and Patents Act 1988.

Pages 7–48 may be photocopied by individual teachers for class use, without permission from the publisher. The materials may not be reproduced in any other form or for any other purpose without the prior permission of the publisher.

Contents

	PoS	page
Introduction		4
Links to the National Curriculum		5

The process of writing

You can do it	W1(a)	6
Stepping stones	W1(a)	7
Ideas in words	W1(c)	8
Thoughts in words	W2(a)	9
Find a beginning	W1(a)	10
And now it's the end	W1(a)	11
Making it look good	W1(c)	12

Skills development

Be an ideas collector	W2(b)	13
Do you really mean that?	W3(c)	14
Using words to paint a picture	W3(c)	15
Similes	W3(c)	16
Rhyme time	W3(c)	17
Making sense	W1(b)	18
It's the detail that counts	W1(c)	19
Making it scan	W1(c)	20
Rhythm	W1(c)	21
A seeing eye	W2(a)	22
Listening	W1(a)	23
Sounds good	W1(b)	24
Sound effects	W1(b)	25
Ppppp poems	W3(c)	26

Forms of poetry

Limericks	W1(c)	27
Haiku	W1(c)	28
Acrostic poems	W1(c)	29
Riddles	W1(c)	30
Cinquains	W1(c)	31
Rondelet	W1(c)	32
Repeat-a-line	W1(c)	33
Poems that go on and on …	W1(c)	34
Story poems	W1(c)	35

Ideas for poems

Families	W1(b)	36
Homes	W1(b)	37
Remembering a first …	W1(b)	38
Feelings	W1(b)	39
Pleasing things	W1(b)	40
Mmm … tastes good	W1(b)	41
Ouch – don't touch!	W1(b)	42
Scents and pongs	W1(b)	43
Nothing	W1(b)	44
Surprise yourself	W1(b)	45
Frighten yourself	W1(b)	46
To the rescue		47

Glossary		48

Introduction

How to be Brilliant at Writing Poetry contains 42 photocopiable ideas for use with 7–11 year olds. The book provides a flexible, but structured resource for developing writing skills, which both you and your pupils will enjoy.

The sheets are self-explanatory and ready to use; the only extra resources needed are a pen or pencil and sometimes extra paper. Word processing on the computer would be a bonus.

How to be Brilliant at Writing Poetry supports many of the Programmes of Study for English in the National Curriculum (see page 5 for further details).

The book is divided into four sections:

The Process of Writing
The sheets in this section are open-ended and focus on the process of writing — from initial idea gathering to redrafting and final product. The sheets recognize that a sense of audience and a purpose for writing are crucial.

It is important that children feel ownership of their poems and are encouraged to share them with a wide audience, both in written and spoken form.

Skills Development
These sheets are designed to be used in conjunction with those in Section 1 as and when needed. Depending on the skills of your pupils, you may wish to use the skills sheets before the process ones, or vice versa.

It is important for the children to be able to practise the skills they have learned and one excellent way for them to do this is to have their own private notebook in which they can experiment.

Forms of Poetry
These sheets provide models for different accepted forms of poetry, for example acrostic, haiku and rondelet. All the models included have an in-built success factor because the simple, but clever structures invite the children to mirror them. Once they've mastered the forms, the children will be able to apply them to any topic ideas, including those given elsewhere in this book.

Ideas for Poems
Basically topic ideas, these sheets can be developed in a multitude of ways. After the initial poems have been written, get the children to share their poems with the whole class. Brainstorm ideas for developing the topic or taking it in a completely different direction. Thus each sheet can provide the basis for several lessons.

Links to the National Curriculum

The activities in *How to be Brilliant at Writing Poetry* allow children to have opportunities to:

1. **Range**
   a. write for varied purposes, understanding that writing is essential to thinking and learning, and enjoyable in itself. They should be taught to use writing as a means of developing, organizing and communicating ideas;

   b. write for an extended range of readers. They should write in response to a wide range of stimuli, including poems, their interests and experiences, and the activities of the classroom;

   c. use the characteristics of different kinds of writing, including imaginative writing. They should be taught to use features of layout and presentation.

2. **Key skills**
   a. write in response to more demanding tasks. As pupils write for a wider range of purposes, they should be taught to distinguish degrees of formality in writing for unfamiliar audiences. They should be encouraged to make judgements about when a particular tone, style, format or choice of vocabulary is appropriate;

   b. plan, draft and improve their work, and to discuss and evaluate their own and others' writing. To develop their writing, pupils should be taught to:

   - **plan** – note and develop initial ideas;
   - **draft** – develop ideas from the plan into structured written text;
   - **revise** – alter and improve the draft;
   - **proof read** – check the draft for spelling and punctuation errors, omissions or repetitions;
   - **present** – prepare a neat, correct and clear final copy.

   Pupils should be encouraged to develop their ability to organize and structure their writing in a variety of ways, using their experience of poetry.

3. **Standard English and Language Study**
   c. distinguish between words of similar meaning, to explain the meanings of words and to experiment with choices of vocabulary. Their interest in words should be extended by the discussion of language use and choices.

You can do it

There isn't just one model for poems. There are hundreds and thousands of models. This means your poem can be exactly the way you want it to be.

You can work at making it the very best you can do. You are allowed to write it and find it doesn't work. Then write it again. And if it doesn't work again, write it another time.

Give yourself permission to not get it right first time! You'll be amazed at how much difference working on it can make!

Choose an idea for a poem. How about one of these?

• zoo • whale • hunger • rain forest • secret island

Write your poem here. Read it aloud to yourself and to a friend. Decide how you could make it better. Work on it here.

Read it aloud to yourself and to a friend. Is it better? What's better about it? Perhaps you could improve it even more. Try again.

EXTRA!
Work with a friend. Talk through each other's ideas, then write your own poems about them. Compare your finished poems.

Read it aloud again.

How to be Brilliant at Writing Poetry

Stepping stones

Sometimes you have to let your mind go wherever it fancies to write a poem. You can be sitting at your desk in school, or at the table at home, or in the garden, or wherever — and your mind decides it wants to be somewhere else. Somewhere real. Or somewhere magical. All you need is a row of stepping stones...

Close your eyes and imagine the stepping stones in front of you. Where are they leading? In your mind, step on to the first stone, then the second, then the third, then.... Keep going until you reach

SOMEWHERE ELSE

Look around at your 'somewhere else' and describe it in a poem.

EXTRA!
When you've finished your stepping stone poem, read it aloud to yourself.
Draw a picture to illustrate your 'somewhere else'.

Ideas in words

Brilliant Poets write about everything under the sun. Sometimes they have good ideas that they want to tell the world about and they think the idea would be better said in a poem than in a story or any other way.

Write your idea first, then turn it into a poem. For example:

An idea like this...

> I think it would be a good idea if we didn't have to go to school every day. We could go on Saturdays and Sundays and have the rest of the week off to play or do more interesting things...

...could turn into a poem like this.

> Two days at school
> And five days off
> What an idea!
> Do not scoff!
> Much less work
> And lots more play
> Good idea!
> What d'you say?

Write an idea here, then turn it into a short poem.

EXTRA!
Swap an idea with a friend and write another poem for each other.

Remember, the poem doesn't *have* to rhyme!

How to be Brilliant at Writing Poetry

© Irene Yates
This page may be photocopied for use in the classroom only

Thoughts in words

A poem lets somebody else read your thoughts. If your thoughts are dull and boring nobody will want to read them. You have to make them alive and 'colourful'.

Instead of thinking in words, think in pictures. Now put the picture into words.

Choose one of the ideas here, get some pictures in your head, and off you go!

EXTRA!
Instead of looking at the picture in your head, look at the picture your words make, and draw or paint it. If your picture doesn't match the one in your head, change the words!

Finding a beginning

Suppose you wrote a poem about an elephant trying to go into town on the bus. You could start with the elephant getting up in the morning, deciding to go into town, wondering whether to go on the bus...

The poem would be much more of a surprise if you began:

Eleanor Elephant
Jumps the queue,
Old men grumble
'How dare you?'
Eleanor grins
And lifts her trunk...

Make some six line beginnings here for:

Wasps attacking a picnic	**Aliens invading the classroom**

Rabbits taking over the supermarket	**Use one of your ideas here**

EXTRA!
Finish the elephant poem on the back of the page. Then choose two from your own beginnings to finish. Why don't you use another page to finish them all?

How to be Brilliant at Writing Poetry

And now it's the end

Brilliant Poets always know where their poem is going to go. That means — what the end will be. Maybe not the actual words, but what kind of ending the poem will have. Maybe it will be sad, maybe funny, maybe dramatic ... but they always know the end.

Here are some endings:

... and then he cried.

... Not me!

... I'll try again tomorrow!

... that's what you think!

... the best news ever!

Choose two endings. Brainstorm what might have led up to the endings. Share your ideas with everybody else, then write the poems.

EXTRA!
Swap poems with someone who's chosen the same endings. Try writing *their* ideas to a different ending.

Making it look good

It makes a lot of difference how you set your poem out.

A host of starlings
In the garden
Took all the bread
Without saying 'Pardon'
Not 'Excuse me. Would you mind?'
And the poor old sparrows
Could find nothing left.

A host of starlings
In the garden
Took all the bread
Without saying 'Pardon'
Not 'Excuse me. Would you mind?'
And the poor old sparrows
Could find nothing left.

A host of starlings
In the garden
Took all the bread
Without saying 'Pardon'
Not 'excuse me'. Would you mind?'
And the poor old sparrows
Could find nothing left.

Choose one of these ideas:

- Lion stalking prey
- Hedgehog coming every night for milk
- Monkeys on the car at the safari park
- Squirrels snatching up all the acorns

Write your poem in not less than six, not more than eight, lines, then fit it into the boxes. Decide which you like best before you write it out neatly to publish it.

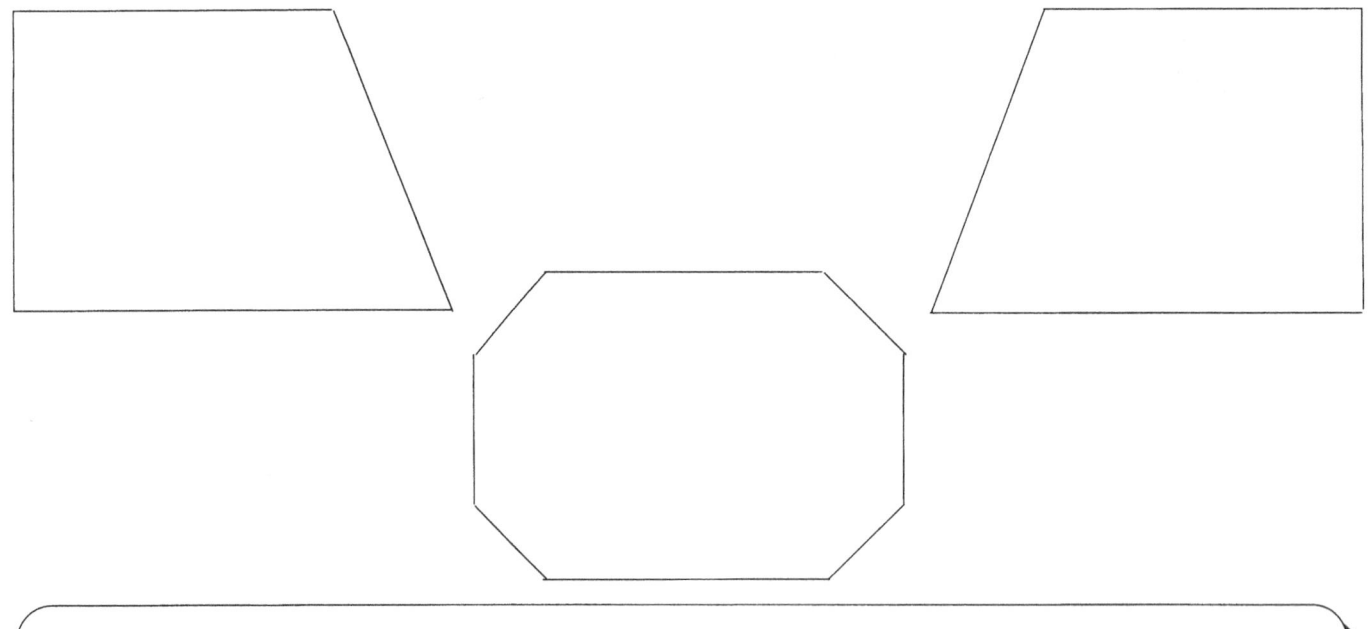

EXTRA!
Find other shapes to write your poems in.
Write another poem from the list and try to fit it into
a triangular shape, or a circular shape.

How to be Brilliant at Writing Poetry

Be an ideas collector

Try brainstorming to get ideas for poems. It works like this. First, choose a topic — say 'animals'.

Think animal — then listen to what's happening in your head and make a note of everything you think. Your animal brainstorm might go like this:

forest   dog   cat   **Animals**   pig   cow   hunting
night   wing   fly   lion
   owl   eagle   predator

You can use any of those ideas either as the subject of a poem, or as words that you can build into phrases and lines.

Do brainstorms for these topics:

Here are some other topics to try: families, water, gardens, colour.

EXTRA!
Turn over the page or get some scrap paper to continue.
Choose two of your brainstorms, and write poems.

© Irene Yates
This page may be photocopied for use in the classroom only.

How to be Brilliant at Writing Poetry

Do you really mean that?

What does he mean when he says his head's splitting? What does she mean when she says 'pick your feet up'? Talk about it with a friend and write your answers here:

My head is splitting means _____

Pick your feet up means _____

These sayings are 'idioms' or 'metaphors'. They don't say *exactly* what they mean, but we all know what they mean. We use them all the time.

Think of some more and write them here. Some are done to start you off.

He lost his temper	_____
She had butterflies in her tummy	_____
Time flies	_____
He's too big for his...	_____
She drives me round...	_____
_____	_____
_____	_____

EXTRA!
Choose one metaphor and draw a
funny picture of it.

How to be Brilliant at Writing Poetry

Using words to paint a picture

Brilliant Poets write in metaphors to make people use their imagination. Metaphors help you to see pictures in your mind.

For example:

> 'Hey you! called the teacher, giving his lion's roar — and the boys ran...

The teacher didn't really have a lion's roar, but the words give you a picture in your mind. Write here what the words tell you about the teacher.

_____

_____

Make up some metaphors here for:

having an argument

eating an ice-cream

breaking friends

getting a surprise

being good

EXTRA! Choose one of your ideas and write a poem using it.

Similes

If you say something is *like* something else, you're using a simile. So you might say:

> Cars roared down the street like hungry dragons

> The road was as bumpy as a roller-coaster ride

> The girl's cheeks were like roses

A simile can use words 'like' or 'as'. Make up some similes of your own to describe:

Tall

Fit

Smooth

Ruffled

Cross

Angry

Pretty

Noisy

Shy

EXTRA!
Similes that everybody knows like 'green as grass', or 'white as snow' are called *clichés*. The trick is to make up new similes that nobody has ever thought of before.

How to be Brilliant at Writing Poetry

Rhyme time

Everyone knows how to make words rhyme. You have to find a word that sounds the same — but the word must make sense!

If you try too hard to make a poem rhyme sometimes you take all the sense out of it and it just becomes silly. For example:

Mad dog, beware
He'll chase you anywhere
And everywhere...

Mad dog over there
without a pear...

Here's the easy way to find rhyming words. Say you wanted to find words that rhyme with 'friend'. Go through the alphabet letter by letter. How many words can you find?

a
b
c
d
e
f
g
h
i
j
k
l
m

n
o
p
q
r
s
t
u
v
w
x
y
z

Keep going to the end of the alphabet. You might find more than one rhyming word for some letters. Make a collection of the words you've found. Now try to find some sensible way to use them to make a poem.

EXTRA!
Make your own rhyming dictionary, and add words to it
whenever you think of them.

Making sense

Fill in the spaces with things that fit.

Taste	Smell	Touch	Hear	See
chocolate	old trainers	mushroom	school bells	colour
	tomato	icicle		clouds

Now move everything along two columns.

Taste	Smell	Touch	Hear	See
school bells	colour	chocolate	old trainers	mushroom
	clouds		tomato	icicle

This is how you might begin the poem:

> The school bell tastes of lumpy gravy in the school hall
> Chocolate feels like velvet on my skin
> My old trainers sound of a million football matches

Carry on until you've got to the end of your lists — then read your poem aloud. You'll be amazed at your imagination!

EXTRA!
Share your poems with a friend, and your friend's poems too.
Move everything along another column and start again.
Then compare your ideas.

It's the detail that counts!

In poems, the smallest details count. Poems with lots of detail are called descriptive poems. Instead of writing:

> it was raining

think about ways to describe what the rain was doing.

> rain bounced off the pavement
>
> it dripped down the boy's back
> it soaked through his anorak
> it squelched in his trainers

Before you know it, you've already got a poem:

> The rain bounced off the pavement,
> Dripped down David's back,
> Soaked through his anorak,
> Squelched in his trainers
> And his wet jeans clung to his knees.

Write your own five lines poems full of details. Try it for:

> There were daisies on the grass

> The football match was nearly up

> The sun shone for our trip

EXTRA!
Think up your own ideas for five line descriptive poems.

Making it scan

Jack and Jill went up the hill
To fetch some clean water in a bucket

Funny, something's wrong there!

It doesn't 'scan' — that's what! If a poem doesn't 'scan' it isn't really a poem at all. It's difficult to explain what 'scanning' means, but if the words trip off the tongue, and there aren't any awkward bits, it means it scans.

With a friend read these lines aloud. Choose which lines scan and put a tick beside them:

☐ One dark night, in the middle of June...

☐ It was on a dark night, sometime about the middle of June...

☐ Oswald the cat, a terrible fiend...

☐ Oswald Cat, a feline terror ...

☐ The name of the cat was terrible Oswald and ...

☐ A terrible cat called Oswald...

Make up some lines here. Make some that scan and some that do not. Swap with a friend and ask them to decide which are which.

EXTRA!
Choose one of your best scanning lines and continue the poem.

How to be Brilliant at Writing Poetry

Rhythm

By using a rhythm you can make a poem dance or jig, or stand quite still. You can make it sound like a train, or gallop like a horse.

The rhythm is the pattern the words make when you say them aloud.

Read these words aloud and tap out the rhythm. Then finish the poems, keeping the rhythm the same. Listen hard to make the rhythm patterns come naturally.

I'm off to London
I'll go on the train

Tiggle, taggle, toggle, tug
Wiggle, waggle, woggle, wug

Feather on sparrow
Sparrow on twig
Twig on branches
Branch on trees

EXTRA!
Tap out a rhythm pattern with a friend, then fit some words to it.
You could take the rhythm of a song you both know.

A seeing eye

Imagine you're the lens in a camera. The camera is pointing.

- Where?
- At what?
- At whom?

Instead of merely 'looking' through the camera lens, imagine that you're watching — or gazing — or staring — or peeping — and write a 'seeing eye' poem about what you can see.

Choose a scene for your camera lens to point at, and write your poem here. Start like this:

> The camera points
> The all-seeing eye watches
> And...

EXTRA!
Poems don't have to rhyme. Write one that does, and one that doesn't.
Read them aloud to a friend. Choose your favourite.

Listening

Listen...
I can hear a Brilliant Poet at work...

Do you know the difference between hearing and listening? Hearing is what you do without trying. If you listen, then you really concentrate on whatever you are listening to.

A good listening experience is to listen to ... silence. If you listen hard you will hear sounds you didn't know were there in the background.

Make a list poem of all the sounds you can hear in your silence, wherever it is.

You could begin like this:

> No sound,
> except my own breathing.
> No sound,
> except...

EXTRA!
When you've finished your silence poem, write a noise poem. Begin the poem like this:

> What a row!
> There is....

Sounds good

Write down all the sounds you can possible think of. Here's a start:

Crashing **BANGING** *whispering* *Whistling* SPLASHING PATTERING

For each word, think of something that might make that sound.
Like this:

Crashing — rocks down a mountainside

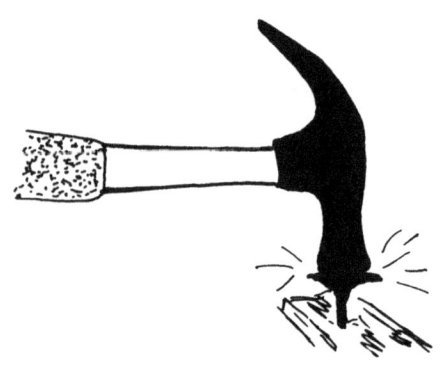

Banging — hammer on a nail

Whispering — wind in the tree tops

EXTRA!
Read your poem aloud, Get a friend to make percussion sounds to go with it so that you make a little sound drama.

When you have something for each word, put them into an order that will make a good poem.

Sound effects

Brilliant Poets love to use words that imitate or suggest the sound they stand for. Words like these are called *onomatopoeia*:

Glug! Bang! Sizzle...

Brrr... Shush!

Imagine the washing going round in the washing machine. Think of the sounds it makes, and try to write them down.

Imagine the sound of a car starting up on an icy morning. Think of the sounds it makes and try to write them down.

Imagine:
- footsteps echoing along a corridor
- clocks in a clockmaker's shop
- stirring a cake
- visiting the dog rescue centre

Now make up some sound words for these ideas and write a sound poem for each one.

EXTRA!
Work with a friend. Read your sound poems aloud to each other.
Can you guess what your friend's poem is about?

Ppppp poems

When you get lots of words beginning with the same sound, it's called *alliteration*.

For example:

> Clive collected crisps constantly

> Outside the slugs slimed

> Rajinder writes rapid rhymes

> Yuck!

Write a poem with alliteration. Here's a start:

>   Mind your manners, Mum said...

or how about

>   The delicate dragonfly danced...

or

>   Wind whispered ...

You choose! Or you can make up one of your own.

EXTRA!
Think of new ideas. Go back to some of the poems you've already written and see if you can change any words to put alliteration into them.

How to be Brilliant at Writing Poetry © Irene Yates

Limericks

There was a young poet at school
Who normally acted the fool
But her poems were brill
When she wrote with a quill
And followed the limerick rule.

And the limerick rule is:

- A limerick has five lines.
- Lines 1, 2, and 5 rhyme with each other.
- Lines 3 and 4 rhyme with each other.
- The rhythm pattern is always the same.
- They're always funny!

Finish these limericks:

Once on a journey to Mars
An astronaut studied the stars
He...

Down in the forest at night
An owl got a terrible fright —
When...

A young boy who thought he was flash
Leapt into the pool with a splash
But...

There was...

When taking...

An old...

EXTRA!
Work out sets of first and second lines.
Swap with a friend and finish off each other's limericks.

Haiku

Haiku is a form of Japanese poetry. It looks very simple, because it's very short. It has three lines. The pattern is:

- the first line has five syllables
- the second line has seven syllables
- the third line has five syllables.

Every Haiku fixes a picture in your mind. For instance:

Sea

Lashing at the cliffs,
striking rocky coves, white-capped
waves dance in anger.

Cat

Purring softly, she
settles on my lap, her paws
padding my jumper.

Now it's your turn! Remember the pattern: 5, 7, 5.

EXTRA!
Read your haiku poems with a friend. Choose some more titles
and write some together.

Acrostic poems

What is an acrostic poem?

A poem
C reeping down the page
R ymes or doesn't rhyme
O bserves interesting ideas
S ays what it likes
T ries to be clever
I t's a kind of word-play
C ome on - it's EASY...

Here's another one:

R akesh plays
A t football,
K icking the ball
E ver so high
S houting 'Yeah!' every time
H e scores.

Write your own acrostic poems here.

G

H

O

S

T

T

I

C

K

L

E

S

N

O

W

S

T

O

R

M

EXTRA!
Write acrostics about your favourite people.

© Irene Yates
This page may be photocopied for use in the classroom only.

How to be Brilliant at Writing Poetry

Riddles

A riddle is a kind of guessing game. Guess what this is:

> It stands in the garden
> Keeping watch.
> It never moves
> Except to do a bit of fishing.
> It has lots of companions
> But no friends.
> Its day never starts
> Its night never ends
> It never straightens
> It never bends
> Just stands in the garden...

Your riddle should give a little bit away, but not too much! It can rhyme or not rhyme, as you wish. Make up riddles for these:

An owl

A computer or computer game

A football team

A hairbrush

Share your riddles aloud with the rest of the class.

EXTRA!
Think of three things of your own to write riddles about.
Get a friend to guess what they are.

How to be Brilliant at Writing Poetry

© Irene Yates

This page may be photocopied for use in the classroom only.

Cinquains

A cinquain has these rules:

- It has five lines
- The first line has one word
- The second line has two words
- The third line has three words
- The fourth line has four words
- The last line has one word.

It can rhyme or not, as you like, but they're usually better if they don't.

Here are some examples:

Grandma

Grandma —
Always laughing
Spoils me rotten
Says I'm her favourite
Ruffian.

School

Assembly
Every morning
In the hall
The headmistress telling us
Off!

The scary thing

Monster
Chasing me
Down the lane
But it's only my
Shadow.

Make up cinquains for:

Favourite games

A birthday party

Your best friend

Your own choice..

> **EXTRA!**
> Decide on a topic and make up a whole series of cinquains about that topic: for instance, five cinquains about school.

© Irene Yates
This page may be photocopied for use in the classroom only.

How to be Brilliant at Writing Poetry

Rondelet

A rondelet is a special kind of poem, with fixed rules. Its rules are:

- It always has seven lines.
- Lines 1, 3 and 7 are exactly the same, with four syllables.
- Line 4 rhymes with line 1 and has eight syllables.
- Lines 2, 5 and 6 rhyme with each other, and each has eight syllables.

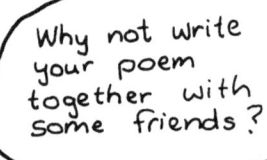

Catch the rhythm from these examples:

> The rain came down
> Like pebbles bouncing off the panes
> The rain came down
> And puddles gathered in the town
> And ditches burst into the lanes
> And rivers bubbled from the drains —
> The rain came down.

> The silent snow
> A velvet blanket on the ground
> The silent snow
> Falling, falling, white and slow
> Drifting down without a sound
> And children watching quite spellbound
> The silent snow.

Write your own rondelets. It might be easier to work in a group to start with, then try the next one by yourself.

Here are some first lines for you to try:

I caught a fish

On Christmas Day

Along our street

I rode the waves

EXTRA!
Choose the rondelet you like best. Copy it out and illustrate it carefully.

Repeat-a-line

When you're stuck, try repeating a line. Like this:

> Far out at sea,
> Far out at sea,
> A dolphin leaps
> In the dancing waves
> And the white foam creeps
> To the hidden caves
> And the sunken wreck
> Keeps its treasure saved
> Far out at sea,
> Far out at sea...

Here are some repeat lines for you to work with. You don't *have* to use them at the beginning and the end. Use them where you think they fit best and write your poems round them.

> Out in the frost,
> Out in the frost

> Out to play,
> Out to play

> Cover your ears,
> Cover your ears

> Tingling fingers,
> Tingling fingers

EXTRA!
Make up some repeat lines of your own. Write your own poems for them, and get your friend to write some too. Then read them aloud to each other and compare them.

© Irene Yates
This page may be photocopied for use in the classroom only.

How to be Brilliant at Writing Poetry

Poems that go on and on

Some poems go round in a circle. They end with the same line as they started with, so they start all over again and go on and on. Like this:

The Poetry Monster

the Poetry Monster's coming today
it's bringing rhymes and rhythms to play
and images and metaphors
and adjectives dripping from its paws —
it's very noisy, smelly too —
it tastes and feels and spills the glue
and gobbles everything in sight
especially words — and loves a fight —
and we said 'Help! Miss, we're all scared!'
and teacher said 'Just be prepared...'
the Poetry Monster's coming today, it's bringing...

You can write poems that go around in a circle about anything.

Start at the beginning and keep going, until you can get yourself back to it.

Use these starting points:

Off into space...

It rained on our trip...

Jenny had a brand new coat...

My mum said...

> **EXTRA!**
> Have a look at some of the poems you've written before. See if you can take the last lines and turn them into circular poems.

How to be Brilliant at Writing Poetry

Story poems

How can it be a poem if it's a story? Well, it can if when you read it aloud it sounds like a poem!

For instance:

Story version	**Poem version**
John and his friend Kate decided that they would do something really exciting on their holiday, have an adventure or something. So they went down to the beach first thing in the morning and...	The two slipped out Early, to the beach, Before the tide was really out, On the lookout for adventure!

Write the story of what happened:

Now turn your story into a poem:

Remember to make it scan. It doesn't have to rhyme. Read it aloud to a friend and listen to see if it goes wrong anywhere. If it does — put it right by juggling the words about.

EXTRA!
Some famous story poems are 'Hiawatha', 'The Albatross' and 'The Raven'.
Get them from the library or ask your teacher to read them aloud to the class.

Families

Families are always good to write about. Because you know them so well, you can write funny things that make them laugh, or nice, loving things, that make them feel appreciated.

Here are some examples. Can you recognize what forms of poetry have been used?

My dad

Always on the hop
From one job to another
Never standing still.

Granny

G ran
R emembers everything
A ll about the old days
N othing's like it used to be
N obody cares any more —
Y es, that's what she always says.

You don't have to write in haiku (like My dad) or acrostic (like Granny), but you can if you want to.

Write about:

Somebody you love a lot.

Somebody who gets on your nerves.

Somebody who gets annoyed with you.

Somebody who thinks you're very special.

EXTRA!
Read your poems to
the people you wrote about.
Write the poem they would
write about you!

Homes

Of course, you know your own home very well, all the nooks and crannies, where everything belongs, all the tidy bits and all the untidy bits.

Begin this poem by thinking in pictures about your home.

Imagine you're taking a friend home for the first time. Write a poem describing your home through their eyes.

EXTRA!
Picture somewhere else you know very well: your classroom, school or club building. Describe it in a poem through someone else's eyes. Make it a someone who's not very likely to go there!

Remembering a first...

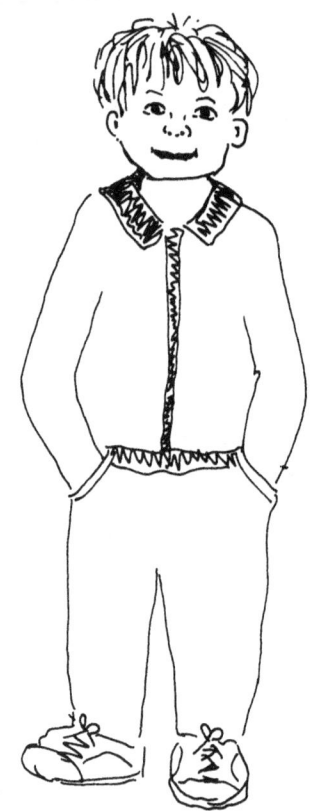

Do your remember your first classroom? Your first day at school? Think yourself back...

All by yourself. No Mum or Dad or brothers or sisters. Only people you don't know. Lots of children. Teachers. Rules. Things to look at. Different smells. Different sounds. Words you'd never heard before.

Close your eyes, think yourself back, and write:

That very first day, I ...

EXTRA!
Remember another 'first'. Maybe the first day you ever went to the dentist.
The first time you played in goal. The first time your best friend came home to tea.
Write the poem (you may need to use the back of the sheet).

How to be Brilliant at Writing Poetry

Feelings

Poems are a good way of exploring your own feelings.

Write down things that make you feel:

good	mad
cross	joyful
bad	lonely
sad	angry

Choose a topic from this list and write a poem beginning with that word. For instance:

> Loneliness is having no one to talk to
> In the middle of the night
> When you can't seem to sleep
> And there isn't any light.
> Loneliness is ...

Start your first poem here:

If you get stuck, repeat the first two words and start again. You can do this as many times as you want to.

EXTRA!
When you've finished one poem, start another one about an opposite feeling. For example, if you did 'Loneliness is...' first, do 'Friendship is...' next. Use the back of the sheet.

© Irene Yates
This page may be photocopied for use in the classroom only.

How to be Brilliant at Writing Poetry

Pleasing things

Make a list of things that make you feel happy. They don't have to be big things. Often the smallest things are the things that make us happiest.

My favourite pebble...

Scoring a goal...

Mum laughing...

Write your list here:

1

2

3

4

5

6

7

8

9

10

Read your list over carefully. Then choose one of the things.

Write a poem which will give your best friend as much pleasure in the thing you've chosen as you have yourself.

Describe your happiness, describe what you've chosen — give your pleasure as a gift to your friend.

EXTRA!
Read your poem aloud to a friend.
Then read out your list to your friend so that they can pick another subject for you to write about.

Mmm...tastes good

How on earth can you describe the taste of something?

It's very difficult. You can say 'fish tastes salty', or 'chocolate tastes delicious' but it doesn't really describe the taste at all.

You really need to think about smell and texture, or find things you can compare with.

For example:

> Trifle is gooey and
> goes round your tongue like
> cement in a mixer, until you
> suddenly reach a strawberry that
> splodges on your teeth,
> sweet and red and soft and before
> you know it's there, it's gone.

Write poems to describe the taste of:

Hamburgers
Fish fingers and chips
Fizzy pop
Samosas
Poppadoms

EXTRA!
Write a poem about the very worst taste of all.

Ouch — don't touch!

Rub your fingers together and try to describe to yourself what they feel like. Difficult, isn't it?

Run your fingers through your hair and try to put into words exactly what the touch of your hair feels like. Even more difficult!

Make a list of all the touching/feeling words you can think of. Here's a few to start you off:

Silky   Tickly
Rough
Spiky
Smooth

Write poems beginning:

Good touch: I like...   Yuck, I hate the feel of...

EXTRA!
Swap touch/feeling words with a friends and write a poem for each other.

How to be Brilliant at Writing Poetry

Scents and pongs

There are good smells and bad smells.

Good smells might be:

... flowers in the garden
... curry sauce at the chip shop
... hot bread in the oven

Mmm... smells good!

Bad smells might be:

...your trainers after walking ten miles
...the dog drying out after falling in the river
...milk when it has gone off

Yuck... smells bad!

Give it lots of thought then choose six good scents, and six bad pongs. Try to find something different from everybody else in the class. Make your poems *different*.

Begin your poems how you like, but end them :

Mmm... smells good!

and

Yuck... smells bad!

EXTRA!
Imagine you had no sense of smell at all. What effect would *that* have on you?
Write a poem about not being able to smell. Use the back of the sheet.

Nothing

People often tell you they're doing nothing, thinking about nothing. But they must be. For a start — they're breathing. The hair on their head is growing. Something must be happening inside their head.

Nothing. Nowhere. No time. No space. No being.

How could you describe it? Is it a black hole? But a black hole is something! Try again!

Begin your poem:

Nothing. Nothing to do...

When you've described that bit write another verse, beginning:

Nothing. Nothing to think about...

Then other verses, beginning:

No time. No beginning or end...

No space. No sides or tops or bottoms...

No being. No body. No mind...

EXTRA!
Imagine a summer day, drifting in space, just being lazy and build the pictures in your mind into a poem.

How to be Brilliant at Writing Poetry

© Irene Yates
This page may be photocopied for use in the classroom only.

Surprise yourself

Make a list of the first ten things to come into your head.

1

2

3

4

5

6

7

8

9

10

Now put all those things together to make a poem! Have fun!

EXTRA!
Work with a friend. Make your list, without thinking about it.
Then swap lists and write a poem from your friend's list.

Frighten yourself

Everybody is frightened of something. Or even, lots of things.

List here ten things you can think of that you're frightened of:

1

2

3

4

5

6

7

8

9

10

Go over the list carefully. Make sure your list really frightens you, then pretend that instead of being frightened of them, you love them. Now write your poem! Have fun!

For example:

> Ghosts? I'm not scared of ghosts.
> Why — I go out looking for them,
> What's better on a windy night
> Than a trek through a haunted forest
> Searching for spirits?

EXTRA!
Share your poem with a friend. Choose from each other's list and write two more poems together.

How to be Brilliant at Writing Poetry

© Irene Yates

This page may be photocopied for use in the classroom only.

To the rescue

This is your chance to show how big and brave you could be if you had to!

Choose one of these ideas:

You're on a boat when you see someone in difficulties in the water.

Or...

There's no one in the street but you and an old lady. The old lady falls down in the gutter. What do you do?

Or...

Nobody lets you in at home and when you look through the window you see — disaster!

Or...

Your friend is being picked on by a gang of bullies. What do you do?

The only rule of the poem is — you must not do anything dangerous to yourself or to other people! Apart from that you can be as brave as it is possible to be.

To the rescue! Off you go!

EXTRA!
Copy out your Super Person poem carefully and illustrate it, showing yourself being heroic.

Glossary

acrostic
Word-play in which the subject of the poem is written downwards, with each letter becoming the first for its line.

alliteration
The rhyme of initial consonant sounds in words. For example: sausages sizzled, lemon liniment.

cinquain
A poem with five lines of one word, two word, three words, four words, and one word.

cliché
A phrase that's been used so many times it no longer has any impact. For example: as green as grass.

haiku
A Japanese form of poetry which has three lines of 5, 7 and 5 syllables, designed to create an image in your mind.

limerick
A five line nonsense poem. Lines 1, 2 and 5 rhyme and lines 3 and 4 rhyme.

metaphor
A comparison, expressed or implied, without the use of 'as' or 'like'. For example: life's but a walking shadow...

onomatopoeia
Imitation of sounds by words. For example: buzz, bang, splash.

presentation
How you make your piece of writing look, for example: neat, coloured in, with or without borders.

rhyme
The similarity between the sounds of words or syllables. For example: cry, buy, lie or community, impunity, opportunity.

riddle
A short descriptive poem without a title so that the listener has to work out what it's about.

rondelet
A poem that has seven lines with set numbers of syllables. Lines 1, 3 and 7 repeat. Line 4 rhymes with line 1. Lines 2, 5 and 6 rhyme with each other.

simile
A comparison which uses 'as' or 'like'. For example: as green as an emerald.

story poem
A poem that tells a story, but isn't a story, because it uses less words than a normal story and has rhythm.

www.ingramcontent.com/pod-product-compliance
Lightning Source LLC
Chambersburg PA
CBHW081349160426
43196CB00014B/2703